# Kunekune Pigs

The ultimate guide for homesteaders and small holders

By Dana Thompson

# Kunekune Pigs

## *The ultimate guide for homesteaders and small-holders*

Publisher: Piwakawaka Valley Ltd     www.piwakawakavalley.co.nz

# CONTENTS

# The History of the KuneKune Pig

These fat little round pigs with upturned snouts are unique to New Zealand. They have been growing in world wide popularity in recent years and are available in both the UK and USA.

The KuneKune (pronounced Kooney Kooney) has a mysterious past. They are very different to the wild pigs brought to New Zealand by Captain Cook, commonly called Captain Cookers for obvious reasons.

Marilyn age 7

Kunekunes appear to share a common ancestor to other Asian pigs, but they are diverse enough to make their heritage a bit of a mystery. Some suggest maybe they were brought to NZ by whalers or traders, however, given the special place of pork in many polynesian cultures, others suggest they were brought over on the canoes (waka) when the original Maori arrived here. There are still some pigs in Polynesia that have tassels on their necks, however they are not closely related enough to say that is exactly where they came from either.

Kune kunes were kept in the traditional settlements, generally left to wander free, but due to their friendly nature and love of food, they stayed close and did not wander far. This is in comparison to a wild Captain Cooker that would happily destroy a human if you got in their way.

Early records did not differentiate the Kunekune from other pigs such as the Captain Cooker and other breeds and crossbreeds kept by the Maori people. So it is probable that they are a mixture of different breeds that has slowly become its own breed.

Kunekune were on the brink of extinction, as the Maori people moved from traditional settlements to the country's growing cities and towns, the old traditions and sadly the Kunekune started being forgotten by many. They were virtually unknown by the white folk that had started to inhabit NZ.

The entire Kunekune population got down to about 50 pigs in 1970 when they were sort of "rediscovered" by Michael Willis and John Simister who were running a wildlife park.

They did all that they could to get as many purebred Kunekune pigs of breedable age from around the country. Then they put in a massive effort to save the breed, implementing a very careful breeding program from just 6 sows and 3 boars.

In 1992 Zoe Lindop and Andrew Calveley took a small breeding group of Kunekunes to the UK to start breeding them there. All KuneKunes in the United States go back to either direct New Zealand or UK imported stock. The USA has imported new Kunekune breeding stock 5 times - in 1996, 2005, 2010, and 2012.

Wilson and Dave with permission from @wilsonanddave.the.kunekunes

# Kunekune Pig Standard

The word 'kune' in Maori means 'fat' or 'round' and that means that 'Kunekune' is doubly so! The Kunekune is known as a 'lard pig' in the same way that the Guinea hog, Potbelly pigs and Mangalitsas. Lard pigs are grown for their meat, and most specifically their wonderful lard. These pigs provide lard for food preservation and soap and salve making in many traditional cultures.

## Overall look

There is a wide range of accepted looks for the Kunekune pig, and this is encouraged among NZ Kunekune breeders to help preserve as much genetic diversity as possible. Because of this, the breed standard is made up of ranges rather than specifics.

Their round bellies and short legs are quite distinct. Image from Mini Haven Kunes

## Size

Kunekunes are small in the world of pigs, but they can still get very large. When compared to commercial pigs, they are definitely smaller. A full-sized adult can weigh between 60 and 200 kg or 120 and 400 lb whereas a full sized commercial sow is usually 400kg (800lb) or more.

Height can vary significantly between different lines, with some breeders preferring the smaller pigs, and others preferring the larger. They can be between 60 to 75 cm ( 24 and 30 inches) at the shoulder, with some lines being even shorter than this.

## Body Shape

The typical Kunekune shape is a short-legged, very short-snouted pig. They have a thick layer of subcutaneous fat giving very rounded body contours. A Kunekune pig has a very different body shape to a commercial pig.

## Upturned, short snout

 Kunekunes have a shortened, upturned nose and a round large head with a dished face, which sounds terrible, but looks very becoming. This feature is unique to the Kunekune, and it does vary in degree of snub angle from one line to another.

The upturned snout of the Kunekune pig means that they are well suited to grazing on grass, and they are usually less likely to root up the ground.

Snout, teeth and mouth should be suitable for grazing grass and free from deformities. Adult boars will have tusks.

## Piri Piri

The wattles or tassels, known as pire pire (or piri piri depending on the local dialect), are about 4cm / 1 ½ inches long, and they hang from the lower jaw. This is one of the variations within the breed - not all Kunekunes have tassels and it is not a showing requirement. However, it is a dominant gene and most breeders will try to breed only tasselled parents, unless they are needing a specific trait from an untasselled breeding animal.

Occasionally piglets may be born with only one tassel, the mother may acciendly lick/bite it off when they babies are born, or sometimes they are not well attached and can be lost through injury.

Tassels are not unique to Kunekunes, and when a tasselled Kunekune is crossed with another breed, the offspring will be tasselled. So while it is a key feature of the Kunekune, it is worth being aware that not all pigs with tassels are pure Kunekune.

## Ears

Kunekune ears can be either erect or floppy, but they should not cover the eyes. They should be inclined forwards. Be sure to check in them for signs of mites or skin conditions.

## Coat

This is another area that can vary significantly among the breed. The most common colours are black, black and white, brown, gold, tan, and cream, sometimes with randomly distributed spots or patches of colour. The Kunekune coat texture can range from short silky hair giving a sleek appearance, to long coarse curls that give a more unkempt look. Adult pigs can sometimes develop a mane over their hackles. Kunekunes also moult and they have a Winter and a Summer coat, sometimes resulting in a marked difference between the two. Extensive hair loss in summer is common, especially in warm areas.

## Disposition

The most important feature of Kunekune pigs is their friendly and gentle nature. Breeders will not breed unfriendly or aggressive animals as this is not seen as a good trait for this breed.

The typical Kunekune nature is a friendly and placid pig that likes close human contact. Kunekunes are intelligent, cheeky, resourceful, and affectionate. Like all pigs they have a real passion for food and they love a good belly or ear scratch.

Boars can be aggressive to each other or if a sow is in season, but generally they will get on well together. Kunekunes are usually very trustworthy, easy to handle, and safe to have children around, even the full sized boars. This is one of the biggest appeals of Kunekunes for homesteaders and smallholders.

## Teacup Pigs or Mini Pigs

Unfortunately, the appeal of a teeny tiny little piggie sitting in a tea cup is too much for some. It is a great way to make money from people that do not know any better. There is no such thing as a mini pig or a teacup pig, and anyone trying to sell you these are untrustworthy and to be avoided.

Kunekunes are very slow to mature, and they can take up to 4 years to reach their full adult size. The final size of a pig is determined both genetically and by its feeding regime. Unfortunately, some people trying to sell mini pigs will give you a strict feeding regime to stick to, and when this is inspected, it is clearly not enough to properly nourish a growing pig. Pigs deprived of enough nutritious food in the growing years will end up smaller than they could have been.

There are ongoing discussions with the New Zealand Kunekune Association about allowing a miniature pig category within the breed.

However, these pigs would have to remain under 50cm (20 inches) at the shoulder after the age of 4 years. While a big this size is small for a pig, they can still easily weigh 100-150kg (200 - 300 lb) depending on their length and condition.

# Are Kune Kune Pigs Right for You

The benefits of keeping Kunekune pigs on a homestead are varied, and it will depend on what you are wanting to get out of having pigs on your homestead whether Kunekunes are right for you.

## The Benefits of Kunekunes

### Small Size

Kunekune pigs are little. While there is no breed standard for size, they are usually about 60cm/2ft tall, but they can vary from 40-70cm even as fully grown adults.

Kunes can weigh from 60-200kg (120-400lb) so there is a vast range in sizes, but even the biggest Kune is much much smaller than a commercial breed pig.

Because they are smaller you can fit more on your land, and they are often kept in small herds or in urban backyards - please check your local rules and requirements though as they are not allowed everywhere. They are also not as intimidating to handle because they are smaller and they need smaller infrastructure to care for them.

### Friendly Disposition

Kunekunes have a very friendly disposition, they are known for their gentleness and even entire males (boars) make really good pets. Because of this, it is possible for homesteaders to keep both a male and a female to breed their own pigs without all the danger of larger aggressive boars being kept on the farm.

Kunekunes that have been raised with regular positive human contact will come running up when called, especially if you have food! Kunekunes will come up for cuddles and belly rubs and they love spending time with their humans.

If you breed your own pigs, you can essentially end up with almost free pigs for the homestead, as well as being able to sell the extras, and know you are helping preserve a rare breed.

### Eats only grass

Kune kune pigs are best raised solely on grass with the odd treat to keep them tame. This is presuming that you have enough pasture to keep them fed. Kunes grow slowly meaning that if you give them too much supplemental feed or too many calories each day then they will get dangerously fat very quickly.

*No one warned us of this when we had a Kunekune when we were growing up. We over-fed Betsy because she begged food off of everyone, and she got so fat her eyelids flopped down and she was blinded by her eyelid fat rolls!*

As we know, pasture raised meat has higher levels of nutrients, less omega 6 fats and more omega 3 fats.

## *Lard*

Kunekunes are a lard pig. That means that they are very fatty, their meat is well marbled with fat and if you overfeed them, they will get overweight and grow huge volumes of back fat very easily. *Betsy, (mentioned above) had 6 inches of fat on her when we got her processed!*

Lard is the creamy soft fat that is rendered from pork fat pieces. It has been used in kitchens for centuries, and it has a unique mix of different types of fats that give it wonderful qualities, especially for baking and frying. If you've never eaten foods cooked with or in lard, you're in for a lovely surprise when you do.

Like most animal fats, lard is higher in saturated fat than most vegetable oils. Lard's reputation was destroyed in the 1960's and '70's when manufacturers persuaded us that Crisco and Parkay, which are vegetable oils that are "hydrogenated" using chemical processes to change the oils to solids, were better choices than traditional animal fats. Then, in the '90s, when the medical establishment began to hammer on saturated fats as the culprits in heart disease, lard's demise was complete.

However, more recent research shows that saturated fat is not the death-food it was once deemed to be, whereas the trans fats found in hydrogenated oils are much worse for us than we realized. It turns out that the trans fats in hydrogenated vegetable margarines and shortenings are lopsided in their ratio of omega-6 to omega-3 fatty acids, and those ratios have been linked to heart disease and that sugar and simple carbohydrates play a lot larger role in inflammation and heart disease than we have been told. This is the problem with allowing Big Ag to buy out our researchers, we have an entire generation (or more) that have been told that natural fats are bad and that grains are good. But that is a story for another day.

Lard has several advantages over other oils/fats, one of them being that it, along with beef tallow, has one of the highest smoke points. That means it doesn't oxidize when you heat it so lard is ideal for high heat cooking.

Also, lard has a high melting point making it the best choice for extra flaky pie crusts and pastries.

Lard has a large variety of uses on the homestead. In the traditional cultures that lard pigs were developed in, they primarily used lard to preserve meats. But it was also used in other cooking and baking as well as to make soaps and salves. See the end of this book for ways you can use lard on your homestead.

### Less mess

Don't be deceived, Kunekunes love mud as much as the next pig, however, they also make a lot less mess than a larger pig would.

Kunekunes are less inclined to root up the ground, and their lighter footprint means that they pug the ground less than their larger cousins.

## Down sides to Kunekune pigs

No animal is perfect, and there are some down sides to Kunekune pigs.

### 1. Slow growing

If you are looking for a quick growing pig for meat then Kunes are not what you are looking for. Kunekunes don't reach full size until about 3 to 4 years of age. However because you are feeding the just grass, it is not costing you more to allow them to grow to size.

They can become sexually mature at around 6 months, but it is considered best to not breed them until they are at least a year old.

## 2. Small

Even a fully grown Kune is not going to be super big, but this makes them easier to handle, and you need less room per pig. Also, if you choose to harvest them yourself,  they are easier to do yourself as you won't need larger winches etc to lift them.

## 3. Very fatty

Kunekune meat is very fatty, they are considered a 'lard pig' which means they are very good fat makers. If you want a lean pork chop then this is not the pig for you.

If, like us, you cook in lashings of healthy, natural lard and you want lard to make soap with, then Kunes are a great choice.

# Kune Kune Care

Kunekunes are very friendly, robust little animals that when cared for well will live for a long time, up to 20 years in some cases!

# Fencing

If you have ever tried to contain a pig, you will know that they are rough on fencing. Kunekunes are no exception. Pigs will lean on, push over, root under and climb over or through many types of fences.

### Solid fencing

If you need to keep your pigs in a small area, a solid fence that is dug into the ground (or filled up with deep bedding) is the solution. This is a good time to use second hand roofing iron, held up with 'T' posts around the whole perimeter.

### Hog Panels

Metal mesh wire similar to that which is used in reinforcing concrete slabs is often sold as hog panels. These lengths of steel are strong and sturdy and can be used between either wooden or metal posts. They are best reinforced with a hotwire inside.

### 7 Wire fences

If you are going to try and contain your pigs behind wire and batten fences, you will need to ensure the wires are extremely tight and are close together, and then cross your fingers.

### Sheep netting/ woven wire

A sheep netting fence will be enough to keep an adult pig in as long as they cannot get under it.

### Electric fences

Many pigs will learn to run at a simple wire or tape electric fence, so you might have better success with an electric netting fence.

If you are planning on using an electric fence of any type with your pigs, it is best to introduce them to it in a small area that they absolutely cannot escape. A solid walled pen with a small length of electric netting or electric tape that they can experience before going out into a paddock that is surrounded by it is the best idea. Give them a few days to a week to learn to leave it alone. Pig netting and tape make a physical barrier, tape or wire make a psychological one that they are less likely to ever want to cross, making moving them more difficult.

### Piglet proof fencing

Keeping in piglets is like trying to keep in rats. They will run under electric and squeeze out through most fences. What we have found that has worked is to run chicken wire around our existing sheep netting fences, bending it over at the bottom so that there is about ½ a foot of netting laying on the ground. Then we used the metal staples that are used to keep weed-mat pegged down to secure it to the ground.

### Gates

Pigs will happily use their brute strength to lift gates clean off their hinges. To prevent this, you can rotate the top hinge bracket (gudgeon) upside down.

### The best fencing option

To keep the pigs best contained, you would use a mixture of two fencing types. 1- 2 strands of hot wire placed inside a permanent fence will slow the pigs down from running through the electric fence, while the electric fence will keep the pigs off the permanent fence and stop them digging under or squeezing through it. This gives you the best chance of keeping the pigs in where you want them to stay.

## Shelter

Kunekunes are well equipped to live outside year round as long as they have sufficient shelter and bedding out in the paddock.

A simple shelter can be cobbled together from some wood pallets with some tin screwed on the roof and around the sides. They need to be able to get out of the wind, rain and sun with enough room for them to move around inside.

A shelter will have enough room for all your pigs to lie in without touching each other. Probably they will choose to snuggle in together, but if they are hiding from the heat in the shade of the shelter, they are unlikely to want to have to be touching.

Kunekunes love to make a nest and they will bury themselves in whatever bedding you supply. Straw or hay makes the best bedding, but be aware they will eat it so it will need replenished now and then.

Although many huts are manufactured without floors, the addition of a heavy plywood floor may help pigs conserve heat. If you're adding huts for the first time, select structures that are portable, easy to clean and of ample size so that anyone who is working with the pigs can get in and move around easily if a sow needs help during farrowing. Shelters that are designed to accommodate several animals usually have drop-down panels for summer ventilation. Make sure the panels can be closed and securely fastened for protection against wind. Ideally, use only new rather than secondhand shelters to avoid the possibility of bringing disease onto the farm.

# Winter Care

Winter temperatures can vary widely, and weather conditions often change rapidly. The first line of defense against rapid changes and cold and damp conditions is maintaining pigs in good body condition prior to winter.

### Feeding in Winter

Kunekunes that consume a quality balanced feed along with pasture are usually well equipped to thrive through cold weather. If pigs are accustomed to getting a substantial part of their daily feed requirement from pasture, make sure you have an ample supply of good-quality hay for winter, it should be leafy and free of mold.

If you are feeding round bales, they should be placed on a stable surface on the flat end to avoid the formation of a donut, which can fall over and smother small pigs.

Be aware that your pigs will snuggle down in the hay and trample plenty of it into the ground, so place bales where hay will compost and benefit the soil of your pasture.

Many farmers take advantage of excess Fall/Autumn produce, such as pumpkins or apples, to supplement pigs' diets. Ask around your friends and community, you might be surprised at what you can find for free or very cheap. Avoid feeding bakery leftovers, the bread and sugar will make the pigs far too fat very quickly.

### *Winter accommodation*

Kunekune pigs really should ideally live on pasture year-round. However, with their tendency to root and destroy paddocks when the ground is super soft and grass is less plentiful means that it is legitimate to want to contain your pigs for the winter in a warmer, drier, less messy, set up.

You can build a simple pen and have their usual shelter inside of it and concrete the floor. This is a simple, easy, permanent option for winter housing for your pigs.

Alternatively, you might choose a 'sacrificial' paddock for Winter grazing. Decide which pastures will be reserved for winter grazing based on accessibility, slope, access to water and convenience. Paddocks that are on a sight hill are ideal for winter because pigs will always have a place that's high and dry. If a particular pasture is already decimated or muddy, it's probably best to avoid using that area until it's frozen or dry. Re-seed it with grass to come away in the spring time.

Kunekune pigs thrive in wooded areas in winter and will happily forage on acorns and other nuts. Wooded areas provide natural windbreaks and can be a valuable part of pigs' winter shelter.

Observe animals daily throughout the cold weather so you're aware of any changes in behavior that may signal illness. Be sure that electric fences are adequately hot and that accumulated snow and ice won't interfere with function. Trim back any long grass that might fall on it while it is wet, this will cause it to short out.

Shelters should be in good condition and without leaks. They should be placed so they face the sun whenever possible. This allows the low light of winter to enter the hut, and prevailing winds will hit the side or back of the structure.

### Deep bedding

Another option is to build another structure (or reuse one you already have) like a carport, green house or pig house.

You would want the air to be able to flow through it, while having a roof over the whole thing to keep the ground dry. You will need at least 30 square feet per pig or 3m2.

You will need the sides to be solid up to about 2 foot high (600mm) at least, with something pig proof above this like hog panels. The sides can be made of treated plywood or roofing iron. In this you will want to add 1 ft / 300mm of wood mulch or wood chips. You can often get these from a local arborist for free or cheap if you can take a truckload delivery.

Each day you should add a little more dry deep bedding to the places the pigs are manuring, you will usually find they choose a corner to make the toilet space. The pigs will root around and have fun in the bedding without making it stinky if you continue to add more dry carbon each day.

At the end of the winter you can either use the bedding on your gardens as an enriched mulch, or pile it up and leave it to compost for a few more months.

As they are not on grass over this time, you will have to feed them a mixture of pellets and fresh foods twice a day.

### *Winter water*

Ensure that water is available in all pastures that your pigs will occupy, and that water lines and pipes are adequately insulated to avoid freezing, or swap to watering with rubber pans that you have to fill up daily.

## Handling

Kunekune pigs are by nature very friendly, however, they can become aggressive if they feel threatened or are hurt. They are large animals, with sharp teeth and are worthy of our respect.

You can keep a full sized boar in the paddock and they are usually just fine with children and other animals, but wisdom would suggest never to leave a child alone with these (or any) large animals.

Regular handling from a young age will have your kunekunes come running when you call them, especially if you have food. Kunes will often roll over for a belly rub and they love being brushed with a horse brush.

You can train your Kunekune to sit when they come in much the same way you would reward train a puppy. Call your Kune over to you and hold in your hand some sort of treat.

Tell them to sit at the same time move the treat from in front of their nose to up over their head between their ears. They will be eager to get the treat and as their nose goes up and follows the treat their bottom will go down and they will sit. Reward them with the treat as soon as they sit down.

If you need to move your Kunekune from one place to another, try coaxing them with a bucket of food. You will be amazed at how easy that becomes once they know your bucket has treats in it.

A pig board or two is another useful thing if you are trying to herd them. Simply hold them in your hands and use them like a wall to block them from turning and to encourage them in a certain direction.

If you need your pigs to go up onto a trailer, make sure the ramp is wide and not steep, under a 20 degree (1 up for every 5 out) slope is ideal. Use a non-slip surface, or add small battens to act as a grip every 8 to 10 inches to stop them slipping.

Small piglets can be carried like you would a puppy, the more secure they feel the less they will squeal. Always wear ear protection if you are handling a pig or piglet that might squeal.

Larger piglets or small pigs can be lifted a short distance by their back legs around the ankle, but be aware they will likely thrash and squeal, not because it hurts but because they don't know what you are doing.

# Feeding

Kunekune pigs should predominantly eat grass. However, some supplemental feeding might be necessary at times.

### *What do Kunekune pigs eat?*

Kunes thrive on a diet of grass, fresh fruit and vegetables. They differ from commercial pigs in that they do not need high levels of protein. Kunes need a maximum of 16% protein, and by preference a little less. They also need much more fibre than commercial pigs.

### *Common Poisonous Plants*

Pigs will eat almost anything, however, they are intelligent animals and it seems that they instinctively know what is good and what is not good for them. Most pigs in our experience will avoid eating toxic plants or parts of the plants. For example, they tend to avoid eating ivy leaves but will readily eat the stems with no adverse effects. However, it is always best to remove poisonous plants from where the pigs will be housed to avoid the animals accidentally eating them. Generally, if humans don't eat it, neither should your pigs.

| | |
|---|---|
| **Yew** (Taxus baccata) <br> **Laburnum** (Laburnum × watereri) <br> **Ivy** (Hedera helix) <br> **Laurel** (not Bay laurel) (Prunus laurocerasus) <br> **Elder** (Sumbucus nigra) <br> **Deadly Nightshade** (Atropa belladonna) <br> **Foxglove** (Digitalis spp.) <br> **Bracken** (Pteridium aquilinum) <br> **Hemlock** (Conium maculatum) <br> Lilly of the Valley (Convallaria majalis) <br> **Ragwort** (Senecio jacobaea) <br> **Buttercup** (Ranunculus spp.) <br> **Spurge** (Euphobia spp.) <br> **Arum Lilly** (Arum italicum) <br> **Periwinkle** (Vinca spp.) <br> **Green/unripe acorns** (Quercus spp.) <br> **Bindweed** (Convolvulus arvensis) | **Cabbage** roots and seeds <br> **Broccoli** roots and seeds <br> **Mustard** root and seeds <br> **Apple** seeds <br> **Young oak** leaves <br> **Tomato** leaves and vine <br> **Avocado** skin and pit <br> **Rhubarb** leaves <br> **Potato** leaves and stems, berries <br> **Green potatoes** <br> **Leaves** of cherry trees, apples, pears, plums and apricots <br> **Bulbs of many plants** (i.e. daffodils, tulips, scillas, hyacinths among others). |

## Grass

Kunekunes should have constant access to grass to graze on. If this is not available, you can supplement with some meadow hay. To minimize rooting in pigs that are prone to it, keep the grass at least 4 inches long. Rotational grazing is a great way to maintain your pastures, reduce parasite pressure and reduce manure build up. Try to move areas every 1-10 days.

## How many Kunekunes per acre

An acre of good, productive pasture can feed up to 6 adult Kunekunes. If your pasture dries out over summer or stops growing over winter, it is recommended that you aim for 3 to 4 Kunekunes per acre and you may still need to supplement feed them.

## Supplemental feed

Kunekune pigs live on grass and vegetables in Summer, in Fall/Autumn this can be supplemented with apples or other windfall fruits.

In the Winter when the grass is less available 1 lb (500g) of 16% protein sow and weaner meal mixed with 1 lb (500g) of grass pellets and hot water into a mash can be given to each adult pig. This amount will vary with the condition of the pigs, lactating sows may require twice this amount. There is also a Pot Bellied pig food on the market that is suitable for Kunes.

If you are raising your Kunekunes for meat, you do feed them differently than if you are raising them to breed. Overweight pigs will not breed well and sows will have trouble during labour if they are too fat. Breeding pigs should be kept lean and fighting fit with a mostly grass diet.

Kunekunes that you want for the freezer should have 1-2 meals a day of a pig grower mix, but just a ½ to ¾ portion - read the instructions on the bag and go from there. Too much feed will get them to put on too much fat, but the extra protein will speed up their overall growth.

### Swill and Scraps

Kitchen scraps can be fed to your pigs, but anything that has meat or eggs in it, be it raw or cooked should be well boiled for 20 minutes to kill any pathogens (this is a legal requirement in many places) and do not feed them bones as they may get stuck in their throat or gut.

### Choking

Kunekune pigs are prone to choking on scraps. Their mouth is set up for grazing and grinding grass up. They have very little dexterity and can choke easily on large pieces of hard food.

Due to their notorious eating behaviour (they eat like pigs, surprisingly), be sure to cut up hard foods to small pieces, apples and carrots in particular as they have been known to cause choking and death in Kunekunes.

Banana peels can also get stuck to the top of their palate causing them to choke, so cut these up smaller before feeding them to your pigs.

Avoid bones all together.

### Waterers

Pigs need a consistent supply of clean, fresh drinking water that they cannot climb in to to muddy up. One of the easiest, and cheapest solutions to this is adding a pig nipple or two to a 50 gallon (200L) plastic barrel. A nipple at 4-6 inches (10-15 cm) off the ground will allow piglets to access it, and another one at 8-12 inches (20-30cm) will allow the adults good access. They will very quickly learn to use them.

You can also get self filling pan systems and all sorts of expensive gadgets, but a cheap and simple nipple in a barrel will suit most owners.

### Bark stripping

Kunekunes with plenty of grass around are less likely to bother existing trees. However, if your trees are young and tender, or the pigs are hungry (or bored) they might find themselves stripping the lower bark off some of your trees. To protect your trees from having their bark stripped you will have to wrap the tree in some heavy gauge chicken wire or similar.

## Rooting and Ringing

*Do Kunekune pigs root?*

Kune Kune pigs have very upturned noses, with some variance amongst the individuals in the breed. These upturned noses, when put to the ground mean that the mouth hits the ground first rather than the nose. This means that MOST Kunekune will not root the ground IF they have sufficient grass to graze on, water to drink and are not mineral deficient.

Some Kunes with straighter noses may root, it does seem to run in some families. They may go through phases of rooting as they are growing up, and will learn to dig for roots and grubs if they are not kept with ample grass (or hay).

Sometimes Kunekunes may benefit from having their nose ringed if they have bouts of rooting up the ground, particularly when there is soft ground after some rain or if there are grass grubs present.

If you are having trouble with your Kunekune rooting up the ground when it is rainy and the ground is soft, you can create a pen to keep them in when they are more likely to be rooting. Over the winter you could keep them in a concrete floored pen with a shelter, or alternatively in a deep bedding situation.

Or, you can put permaculture into action and make your problem your solution, get those piggies digging up your new garden bed.

### How to ring a Kunekune's nose

It is considered best practice to get your vet in to sedate your pig, give local anesthetic and place either a series of

clips over the top rim of the snout, or for more insistent rooters, one thick ring through the middle of the nose may be placed.

It is possible to apply clips yourself, you can buy the clips which are simply a 'C' shaped piece of copper or stainless steel thick gauge wire, and the applicator pliers for reasonably cheap from farm supply stores.

You should aim to place the clip through a nostril, over the nose plate/rooter and into the soft tissue behind it. You will need one at 10 o'clock, one in the middle at 12 o'clock and one at 2 o'clock.

You will need someone to hold down the pig, and someone that has strong hands to squeeze the pliers. This is much easier to do on a smaller younger pig.

It is worth noting that ringing a pig may not stop the rooting behaviour, and some will simply continue to root and the clips will fall out. For others, it is enough to stop them from rooting, and they stop the habit.

# Wallowing

Pigs love to wallow, and Kunekunes are no exception to this. If you are keeping your Kunekunes in a paddock where water pools, they will very quickly turn it into a mud bath.

Wallowing helps to keep the pigs both cool and clean. The mud dries up and removes excess skin oils, it helps keep insects and annoying bugs away, can act as a sunblock and it cools them down when it is hot.

If you do not have land that you would happily sacrifice as a wallow, you can spend some time on a hot day hosing the pigs off. Most will love a good shower in the heat of the day. They will not toilet in a mud wallow as long as they have enough room to avoid it, and it is considered a normal and healthy part of being a pig. If it is possible to allow them to have a wallow, it would be appreciated by them and of a benefit to their wellbeing.

# Health and Maintenance

Kunekunes are robust little animals that are generally hardy and seldom get ill. With some simple routine maintenance most major illnesses or disease can be avoided.

Just in case, have a place prepared for sick animals well ahead of Winter. Make sure you can move animals to the area without undue stress or injury to the pigs or the person moving them.

## Weight

Kunekune pigs live up to their name. They really are pigs. They will eat anything and everything (and far too much of it) if they are allowed to. A healthy sized Kunekune will be rounded, but be able to freely run. Their belly should be well clear of the ground, and they should have some sort of inclination towards having a waistline.

An overweight Kunekune can develop chronic health conditions, much like a human can. Kidney disease, heart disease and diabetes can all affect them. Morbidly obese animals can develop eyelid folds that render them blind.

To avoid getting overweight, it is recommended that your Kunekune predominantly eats grass. Kunekunes are the only true grazing breed of pigs, so their unique requirement for grass is an important part of owning them and keeping them healthy.

This is Miss Piggy after being rescued, she was fed bakery scraps

Same piggy after eating a proper diet, Photos from Mini Haven Kunes
(note the winter and summer coat difference as well!)

# Grooming

Despite all their hair, Kunekune pigs don't really need to be groomed. However, that is not to say they wouldn't love you to give them a good brush down now and then. A plastic, short bristle horse brush is perfect to give the pigs a good scratch and rub down without wearing out the skin on your hand.

## Teeth

Kunekune's teeth can be a problem. In some lines of genetics teeth and jaw malformations are more common than others. Breeders are working hard to remove these genetics from the breeding pool.

Male kunekunes will grow tusks as they reach their full mature size at between 2 and 4 years of age. These seldom cause problems, but they can be surgically removed if required.

Giving your Kunekune's plenty of fibrous grass to chew and less starchy grains will help keep their teeth free of dental disease.

## Tassels or Wattles

A classic look of the Kunekune is the tassels, wattles or piri piri that hang from their necks. There is nothing you have to do to care for these, they are just excess blobs of skin. If for some reason they get damaged, caught on something or injured so that they are bleeding then you should treat them as you would with any other open wound.

## Nails/hooves

Kunekunes may need their hooves trimmed occasionally. You can give them access to a concrete pad and often the friction from walking on this is enough to keep them filed down. Otherwise, you can have one person giving your pig a belly rub while the other uses goat hoof trimming shears just to trim off the long hard pieces of nail that are causing the problem.

On lighter colored pigs it is very easy to see the excess hoof growth that needs to be cut as you can easily see their nail bed. You will want to trim as close as possible to the nail bed without actually cutting into it as not only will it bleed, but it will hurt too.

You want their hoof to be flat on the bottom with no excess growth on the sides or front of the foot. With darker colored pigs it is hard to see the nail bed so you need to be more careful with them. You should just trim slowly and don't go past your comfort zone on pigs with black feet. You can trim the excess growth away and then use a file or a Dremel type tool to smooth the edges if you like.

If your pig won't willingly lie down, you will need a couple of spare humans to help flip your pig onto their back with their legs up in the air. Without access to the ground to push off of you will find they will be less likely to be able to escape when all 4 feet are up off the ground. But be sure to wear ear protection!

# Worming

Worm infection of pigs generally does not cause dramatic signs of disease but effects can be less obvious and can result in thin sows, increased mortality rates in young litters, reduced growth rates and liver condemnations at slaughter.

Because Kunekunes are kept outdoors, they are at greater risk of infection, as worm eggs contaminate the soil and some roundworms even use the earthworm as an intermediate host. Pig paddocks can stay infected for years once they have been contaminated.

### *What worms infect pigs?*

There are a variety of worms that affect Kunekunes, and they do vary from country to country. Here are some of the most common:

### Red stomach worm (Hyostrongylus rubidus)

Mainly found in adult pigs, symptoms generally most noticeable in lactating sows. Causes weight loss "thin sow syndrome" reduced fertility and reduced piglet birth weights.

## Nodular worm (Oesophogostomum spp)

This is the most common worm found in the UK pig population. Also contributes to "thin sow syndrome". Infection may also make secondary infection with swine dysentery more likely. Numbers of worms rise markedly around the time of farrowing, exposing the piglets to high infection risk. It is important to worm the sow shortly before farrowing to prevent these.

## Large roundworm (Ascaris suum)

This is the largest gut parasite of pigs and can reach 400mm in length. The greatest damage is done by the larval stages, as they migrate through the lungs and liver. This can cause pneumonia in young piglets and is the cause of "milk spot liver", seen at the abattoir. The eggs last for years in the environment and the best method of control is by worming all the stock twice a year.

## Whipworm (Trichuris suis)

This lives in the large intestine and is not very harmful itself but may predispose to secondary gut infections.

## Lungworm (Metastrongylus apri)

Adult worms live in the airways of the lungs and cause coughing and reduced growth rate. This worm has been rare but is becoming more common as more pig herds are kept outdoors.

### How do you diagnose worm infections?

The best way to check any animal for worms is to do a fecal smear count. This is because very few infections are obvious from the outside of the pig but a faeces sample, taken to your vet, will detect eggs passed by the adult worms in the pig's gut and they can get an idea of the worm load.

### How to treat worm infections

Your local vet will be able to advise on exact treatment programmes but most wormers can simply be given in feed.

### When to worm your Kunekunes

Pigs should be treated on arrival to your property before they meet your other pigs. Young piglets will need more frequent treatment, ask your vet for the best worming protocol for your area and the time of the year, usually it is at 4 weeks and 8 weeks at weaning, and at 12 weeks.

Treat all adult pigs including your boars every 4 to 6 months as well as treating a pregnant sow 2 to 3 weeks before farrowing and 7 days before going to the boar.

Hygiene is also important in the control of worm infections. Clean and disinfect buildings between groups of pigs, rotate the use of outdoor paddocks and avoid spreading the manure on land that may house pigs unless it has been very well composted.

## Healthy Pig Facts

### Temperature

A pig's temperature is 102 Fahrenheit or 38.89 Celsius. Take a pigs temperature by gently inserting the thermometer into their rectum; a bit of lubrication will help it go in. Keep enough of the thermometer between your thumb and forefinger to be sure you don't let go then wait about a minute and a half before withdrawing it to read.

### Heart rate

A pig's pulse is 70 to 80 per minute

### Breathing

A pigs respiration rate is 20 to 30 per minute

### Reproduction

A sow cycles every 3 weeks

A sows gestation period is 108 to 120 days.

A sow will come "hogging" to the boar 4 to 7 days after her piglets have been weaned to be re-bred if he is around.

## Giving an injection

All vaccines and medications should be stored as per manufacturer's instructions, most often this means in the fridge, NOT the freezer. To draw the medication or vaccine from the bottle when injecting more than one pig, insert a sterile needle into the bottle and use separate sterile needles to inject each pig.

To inject subcutaneous means under the skin, in the pig this means in the neck tight up behind the ear. To inject intramuscularly as the word suggests, directly into the muscle, the hams are a good spot on a pig.

# Diseases

## Respiratory Diseases

There are a range of viruses and bacteria causing pneumonia, bronchitis, and nasal cavity infections in Kunekunes. If you notice rapid or laboured breathing in your pig, it is very unwell, and needs immediate treatment by a vet. Coughing may be caused by bronchitis or pneumonia but may also be due to lungworm infection.

It is possible to vaccinate against Atrophic Rhinitis with A-RT vaccine, but it is generally not necessary. It is best to keep your pigs in adequately ventilated, but not draughty huts or buildings and separate any infected animals immediately. If your pigs develop a cough, be sure to get the vet out quickly as they seldom complain about feeling sick until it is quite late, and pneumonia will kill a pig very quickly.

## Parvo-Virus

This virus has been known for many years to cause reproductive failure, infertility and mummified foetuses in sows, but these symptoms can also be caused by other factors.

You can vaccinate against Parvo-Virus. However, it is recommended to not vaccinate against parvo virus unless a material blood test is submitted to a veterinary laboratory first. The vaccine is expensive and the small pig keeper with just one or two breeding sows is highly unlikely to have parvo in his/her herd.

## Arthritis

Arthritis is a condition of swollen, sore joints. Often older animals (including humans) can develop this in older age.

To minimise the risk of developing arthritis encourage your pigs to move around and get some exercise to keep their joints mobile. At the same time try to avoid excess weight gains. If the arthritis is affecting their quality of life you might like to get some alternative treatments to go alongside the vet prescribed pain relief. Many old piggies like a massage, a bath in nice warm water or heat packs on their sore old joints.

Natural supplements that can help in some situations include glucosamine, chondroitin, turmeric or curcumin and fish oil. Be sure to check with your vet before giving any alternative medications to your pigs. Inflammation caused by grain based diets might also be to blame, so removing grain based treats from their diet might also be beneficial.

## Diarrhoea / Scours

Diarrhoea in your Kunekune can be caused by dietary upsets or infections, and in some cases (such as in very young piglets) it can be so severe or serious that it is life threatening. A scouring piglet needs to be treated immediately. They will lose condition very quickly, and often it is not obvious to spot until it is too late. Because piglets die so quickly from dehydration, keep an eye out for wet tails on your twice daily checks of the litter.

A vet will usually rehydrate the piglet with intravenous fluids, and you can get the hydration started by giving electrolyte water by mouth while you are waiting for the vet.

If you do not have any electrolytes at home, you can use some slightly warm boiled water where you have added ½ teaspoon of salt and 2 teaspoon of sugar per cup of water. Carefully use a small spoon or syringe to dribble it down the throat of the piglet, this should help to keep it going until your vet arrives.

Scouring in a weaned piglet is often due to overfeeding, a change of diet or housing them in cold draughty conditions. It is not as likely to be the result of E. Coli unless hygiene is very poor.

There are infectious causes for scouring which include E.Coli, Coccidiosis, Rotavirus and other miscellaneous viruses and bacteria, can cause a serious outbreak with whole litters affected or wiped out. If pigs are quieter than normal, have a reduced appetite, or have blood in the diarrhoea, they need prompt veterinary treatment with antibiotics and electrolytes.

### Dietary causes

A sudden change in diet, eating something that they shouldn't, undiluted milk, or too much fat in the diet can cause a bout of diarrhoea.

### Infectious causes

E. coli bacteria scours, Rotavirus and other miscellaneous viruses and bacteria can cause scours in your pigs. Infections can cause a serious outbreak with the whole litter affected. Be sure to wash your hands well, as many of these can also affect humans.

### Internal parasites

In rare cases internal parasites can cause diarrhoea, but are usually only a contributing cause and not the main cause of the scours.

If you notice that your pigs with diarrhoea are quieter than normal, have a reduced appetite, or have blood in the diarrhoea, they need prompt treatment with antibiotics and electrolytes.

## Leptospirosis

This infection can cause kidney problems, generalised illness, or if a sow develops the infection during early pregnancy she will abort her pregnancy. Although infections of the Leptospirosis bacteria are not common in pigs, it is recognised as a health hazard to people dealing with pigs and cattle and pigs are usually vaccinated against it.

## Abortion

If you notice a lost pregnancy, there are 3 main infectious agents that can cause abortions or the birth of very weak piglets

- Parvovirus
- Toxoplasmosis
- Leptospirosis.

Where a large number of pigs are kept together, it is often advisable to vaccinate against both Leptospirosis and Parvovirus.

There are some toxins of certain fungi in cereal-based food can also cause abortions. Always handle any stillborn piglets or aborted material with care because of the risk of infecting yourself or others with whatever the mother was affected by.

## Mastitis

Mastitis is the infection of the mammary glands, and it can occur before or after farrowing. The classic symptom of mastitis is the glands are swollen, hot and painful. Farrowing time and weaning time are the most common times that mastitis occurs. Prompt treatment with antibiotics is needed to clear the infection quickly or an abscess may form needing surgical intervention. A pig may also  sepsis (blood infection, often fatal) if mastitis is left untreated. Following mastitis there is usually quite a reduction in the amount of milk produced for a while until it builds back up, and there may not be sufficient milk for the piglets if the mastitis occurs soon after farrowing.

# Skin Conditions

## Parakeratosis

Parakeratosis is a nutritional deficiency disease of 6 to 16 week old pigs characterized by lesions of the superficial layers of the skin. It is a metabolic disturbance resulting from a deficiency of zinc or inadequate absorption of zinc due to an excess of calcium, phytates, or other chelating agents in the diet. Pigs present with browned dry patches with thick flakes of skin which progress to deep dry skin fissures, and can also be lethargic and off their food.

Treatment includes using a zinc cream to aid healing and an increase of zinc and calcium in the diet.

# Fistulas

Kunekune pigs can develop facial fistulas after an abscess. A fistula is a hole from one place to another, in this case from the mouth to the outside of the pig's face.

There has been some research done into the jaw malformations and the resulting fistulas that can occur in the Kunekune population. The fistula problem seems to be a result of the way the teeth are not meeting properly allowing food to build up in a pouch which then develops an infection that tracts through the skin to the outside of the pig's face where it presents as an abscess.

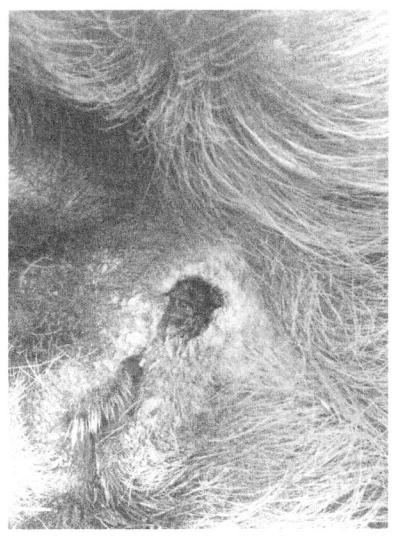

These abscesses will need vet attention, they will need to be lanced, drained and flushed to keep them open and clean. A course of antibiotics is usually required to clear up the infection. If the fistula is left open, and the inside heals up well, a pig can live with this for many years, think of it like a piercing, it stops hurting once it heals even if the hole remains. If the abscess closes over it is likely it will continue to get infected and re-abscess occasionally.

Many vets are not aware of this situation and it is recommended that you mention the rare condition to them and suggest they do some research into it and the best mode of treatment.

## Ringworm

Ringworm is not a worm but a fungal skin infection. It is not common in pigs, but if you have hedgehogs or other known wild carriers in your area, they can pick it up. It shows as a round, red, itchy patch and can be easily cleared up with some anti-fungal cream from your vet. Be sure to wear gloves when applying it and wash your hands well as it is very contagious and humans can catch it.

## Lice

Lice are host specific, so pigs will only get pig lice breeding on them. The lice are large and brown and move around when disturbed. The lice lay their eggs on the hair on the sides of the lower neck and at the back of the legs, the eggs look like cream spots stuck to the hair. Treatment is topical insecticide such as a louse powder or alternatively an Ivermectin injection.

## Ticks

Ticks can be a problem over summer, and in areas with Lymes disease it is worth noting that pigs can be affected by Lymes. There are many ways of removing ticks, but do not pull at them as it leaves their heads buried in the skin, increasing the risk of infection. Treat with a topical drench, neem oil spray or ivermectin. Guinea fowl are often kept to keep the tick population down.

Ticks behind the ear

## Mange

Mange in Kunekunes occurs mainly in summer, and it looks like crusty reddened (often balding) areas especially around the head and legs. Adults tend to build some immunity to it, however piglets  can end up with dry crusty areas all over their body. They also have general symptoms of a poor growth rate failure to thrive. Treatment is topical insecticidal wash or Ivermectin injection.

## Greasy Pig Disease

Greasy pig disease is a bacterial infection of the skin, mainly in young pigs in warm humid climates over the summer or rainy season. Their skin is red, crusty and weeping, and often the piglet shows generalised poor health. Treatment is antibiotics and topical antiseptics and it is best to see your vet to confirm

# Keeping Kune Kunes as Pets

Kunekune pigs do make great pets. There is a growing movement in New Zealand of people keeping Kunekunes as pets, even letting them into the house.

They are an unusual choice as a house pet, but Kunekune pigs are naturally clean animals and they can be trained much like a dog.

## Toilet Training

Your piglet will need to go to the toilet when she wakes up, after a drink and after her food. Everytime she does one of these things, take her through the door that you want her to ask to go out of, and take her to the spot you want her to toilet. Wait for her to do her business and when she does, reward her with lots of praise and a small food treat. A single grain-based pig nut will suffice. Keep an eye on Miss Piggy while she is in the house, and as soon as you see her go towards the out door, praise her and let her out.

## Teaching Tricks

You can train your Kunekune to do most things that a dog can do. Be sure to keep training sessions short, less than 10 minutes. As soon as your pig is losing interest, you should stop and try again later.

Use lots of praise and small food treats to reinforce good behaviour. A simple, stern "Uttutt" or a "no" is enough to tell them that they are doing something wrong. Avoid physical punishment, as a scared pig can become a dangerous pig.

Tucker using the slide to get off the garden

## House Manners

You should expect your house pig to have the same manners as you would expect a dog to have. No jumping on people, restraint around meal times, to sit for pats and to ask to go outside to the toilet.

Diego sitting with his mate Devon

The younger you start training these manners, the easier it will be for them to learn the rules. Pigs naturally live in a social structure and they

can learn what is expected of them within the social group, but this will be easier for them to adopt while they are young.

# Keeping Kune Kunes for Pork

If you are keeping your Kunekunes on a homestead, you might be considering keeping them for pork or bacon. Their pasture raised meat is excellent, and their friendly disposition makes them easier to raise. Remember pigs, even ones destined for the freezer need a paddock mate, you should not keep one pig by itself, and when it is slaughter day, be sure not to leave one alone in the paddock for more than a few hours. Either add another piggy friend, or process them both on the same day.

## A mental choice

Kunekunes are cute, and endearing, and friendly, and fun and they can wrap themselves around your little finger and make their way into your heart. What I am trying to say is, you need to decide if realistically you can let your pigs become bacon.

On our farm we deal with this by having the breeding pigs as pets and the meat animals are raised in a separate area where we spend less time bonding with them. They are also fed differently, so it actually makes sense to keep them separated.

If you are concerned that you may get too attached to your pigs before they go for slaughter, it really is worth deciding from the outset that you won't give them names and perhaps even choose piglets whose pattern or colours don't appeal as much as others.

## Size Matters

Kunekune pigs come in such a range of sizes. Obviously they are all made of meat, and you can eat any of them. However, if you are going to all the effort of slaughtering and processing a pig, it makes sense that you are using the bigger animals for this.

If you have the choice of choosing a piglet to raise for the freezer, or as foundation stock to breed your own 'bacon seeds' (piglets to raise for the freezer) it would be best to choose the larger, faster growing animals for this job. Kunekune come in a multitude of colours and sizes, and whilst the size of the sow and boar is not a guarantee of the piglets finished size it can give something of an indication. If you're hoping for chops and bacon look for a nice length of back to the piglet. Ideally the piglet will be chunky and healthy.

## Feeding

Kunekune pigs do get fat very easily. They specialise in convincing their owners that they are starving and must have more feed even if they were only fed 5 minutes earlier. It is not good for any pig to be overfed, but if you are rearing for meat the feed you choose, and the volume they receive will have a large impact on the resulting meat that is produced.

Extra feed for a Kunekune does not result in more meat, but it will make them lay down more fat, and you are more likely to end up with lower quality meat with considerably more fat both marbled through it and as a thick layer around the outside.

Kunekune pork is often described as sweet, and this is enhanced by their grazing diet and comparatively slow growth. To allow for muscle development which will become succulent pork, they also need to be relatively fit and active.

Kunekune can be raised on good quality grazing without need for supplementary feeding while the grass is growing well. Be aware that the grazing does need to be of an adequate quality to provide the nutrients that they need.

Growing Kunekunes will grow best if their feed (including grass) is around 14-16% protein. If your grazing is of poor quality, you can add in ½ a pound or 250g of feed once or twice a day to ensure they are getting enough protein to grow quickly.

If you do feed commercial pellets, these are readily available from livestock feed merchants, smallholder suppliers and farm stores. They are usually called 'sow rolls' or 'sow and weaner pellets' and there are many brands available. When grazing is poor or the weather is not supporting good growth you will need to feed them a supplementary pig feed.

Kunekunes are not commercial growing hogs. Most pig feeds on the market are aimed at commercial pigs and have names like 'grower' and 'finisher'. These are primarily aimed at the fast growing commercial market to support and enhance very fast growth. But in a Kunekune pig, fed at the recommended rate as stated on the bag are likely to just make for fat overweight little Kunes.

For most homesteaders or smallholders, the choice of Kunekune has been influenced by their very low feed costs and there is really no need, or benefit, to buying expensive branded life stages feed which is less suited to the slower growth rate of the Kunekune.

They will also appreciate vegetables and fruit. Carrots and sugar beet are often readily available from feed merchants or local farms and can provide variety and fibre. Apples, pears, plums and cabbage from supermarket scrap bins or damaged items from market gardeners are well enjoyed by pigs.

### *Water*

A constant supply of clean fresh water is essential for all pigs. A lack of clean water can make a significant difference to the quality and quantity of meat you will get, not to mention the comfort and quality of life of your pigs.

Your Kunekunes need water to enable their basic bodily functions and growth. Contaminated water can lead to illness or even death. Make sure that you have a way to water your pigs well before you purchase your piglets. This can be a tank storage system or mains fed, but whatever system is used you will need a trough or drinker that is accessible and robust, and a means of keeping the supply clean and able to be used at all times.

## Medications

You will need to keep careful and accurate records of any medications you give to your pigs, including wormers, and this applies to pigs being reared for meat as well as breeding or pets. Some medications cannot be used for pigs that are going to become part of the food chain, so always check with your vet before giving any medication. There is usually a 'withholding period' associated with medicines which gives the minimum timeline between when a medication can be given before the pig can then be slaughtered for human consumption. It is very important to adhere to these withdrawal periods, so keep good date records.

## Choosing an Abattoir

There are two ways to end raising pigs for meat at home. One is to send the pig away to an abattoir and butcher and have it come back as ready to eat meat. The other is to do it all yourself at home.

If you choose to process your pig at home yourself, it is strongly recommended that you have someone who has done it before to come and help you with at least your first one or two until you are sure you know what you are doing.

It is a good idea to contact the abattoir you are thinking of using well before the date you have chosen to take your pigs. Which abattoir you choose and how you experience it may significantly affect how you feel about the whole process of raising and butchering your own pigs, so it is worth taking the time to become familiar with what happens and who is going to be doing this for you.

Pigs are negatively affected by stress and need to have as little stress as possible during their transport and when arriving. They will pick up on your stress and it will add to theirs. So try and stay cool, calm and collected. Allow plenty of time and try not to rush. You will need a livestock trailer to transport your pigs to the abattoir, which has loading gates and a ramp to get them up onto it.

Many abattoirs will allow you to visit before butchering day. Look for an environment that is appropriately clean, with staff that treat the animals with respect and consideration. There is usually an animal health inspector and/or vet on hand in most places.

If your pigs have ear tags, it is a good idea to check what type of ear tags that the abattoir will accept, as some will only accept metal 'slaughter' tags, others will accept the plastic tags. Your pigs will need to be tagged with your herd mark, either with ear tags or 'slap marks' which is a paint.

Don't assume there will always be space for you, as many abattoirs are very busy and you will need to book well in advance. When you drop your pigs off they will be moved into a holding pen where they will remain for a very short period of time before slaughter.

You might be able to find a smaller processor that will come out and shoot your pig on site for you and then take them away to finish the butchering process. Different countries have different rules and expectations around this, but your local butcher is likely a good place to start asking around what is usually done where you live.

Before taking your pigs to be slaughtered, have a think about what you want back in terms of meat. Many abattoirs have their own butchery, but if not you will need to arrange for the carcass to be butchered if you are not planning to do this yourself.

The abattoir will probably be able to tell you the name of a butcher if you have not selected your own, and can usually arrange transport of the carcass if necessary.

You can usually choose from a very basic kill and get the whole carcass back to butcher yourself, or to a full service where they will make sausage and bacon for you along with joints, chops etc. If you're not sure what you want, talk to the butcher beforehand. You will also probably have the choice of whether you want the head and any offal back or not.

It will usually take a few days after dropping your pigs off at the abattoir to when the meat is actually ready. In a kunekune the meat is darker than commercial 'white' pork so don't be alarmed if it looks different to the very pale pork you usually see in the supermarket.

## Butchering your Pigs at Home

If you decide to process your pigs at home, you will need a rifle or shotgun, a long small, sharp knife to stick/bleed the pig and a way of lifting it up. Kunekunes are very hairy, so it is common to skin them, in which case a skinning knife is very helpful. If you chose to scald and scrape the pig you will need a hot bath or barrel of water to dunk them in and a way of lifting them in and out.

If the logistics of this hasn't put you off, here is what you need to do.

## *Slaughter*

Keep your pig off feed and water overnight, and bring them a shallow pan filled with milk or milk/water combined to drink from. A pig that is eating throws its head and body all over the show, but a drinking pig will keep its head still.

If you have a friendly pig and a shy pig, take the shy pig first, the friendly or bold pig is more likely to come and stand still again later, whereas the shy one without its confident friend may not.

Use a rifle or shotgun with a large bullet to stun the pig and stop conscious brain activity. This should be done by someone that is confident at shooting pigs, as a mis-fire can go very wrong and cause unwanted pain to the pig. Pigs are some of the most difficult to shoot, and with the Kunekune's

dish shaped face, they are even more so. The brain is small, and quite deep in the head.

The ideal site for shooting pigs is one finger's width above eye level, on the mid-line of the forehead, aiming towards the tail.

Some older pigs, especially boars, may have a bony ridge running down the centre of the forehead. If this is the case, put the barrel of the gun slightly to one side of the ridge, aiming into the centre of the head. Because of the problems which might arise with adult pigs, it is recommended that where possible, they are destroyed by use of a shotgun (12, 16 or 20 bore).

Alternatively the animal can be shot through an eye, or from behind an ear, aiming toward the middle of the head.

Be sure to keep a shotgun 5-25cm (2-10inches) away from the pigs head.

Once the pig has been shot, you must move immediately to sticking/bleeding the pig while its heart is still beating. You can do this either in the neck, or in the chest.

Sticking in the neck:

Under the ear, towards the lower portion of the neck, stick the knife in 4-6 inches and cut round under the head around to under the other ear severing the arteries as you go.

Sticking in the chest:

Put your knife in just in front of the breast bone and angled back towards the pig at about 45 degrees. Force it down and back to a point about 15cm below the breastbone. Twist it and cut back towards the head about 5cm (2inches). This should sever the main branching arteries without puncturing the chest cavity.

Though your pig is quite dead by now, you will probably notice it to start to thrash. This is normal and it is all the nerves firing as they are shutting down.

### *Skinning or scalding*

It is up to you whether you want to attempt skinning or scalding. To scald you will need a container big enough to hold your whole pig and a way to get the water up to 65C/ 150F and keep it there.

Either way, you will need to hang the pig up. Using a gambrel attached to a chain on a pulley or attached to the arm of a tractor. Make a cut between the bone and the tendon just above the ankle on both back feet and insert an end of the gambrel into each side.

If you are scalding and scraping, you should then raise the pig up and slowly dunk it into the hot water, keeping it moving so as to not scald the skin. Keep checking the hair and when it pulls off easily, you can lift the pig and lower it on to a firm, clean surface to scrape it. Ideally you would have a purpose-made scraper, but if you do not, you will need a blunt, but strong metal edge. For stubborn patches of hair, pour more of the hot water over several times with a pot.

To skin, you should start at the back hocks and slowly work your way down the body, leaving as much fat on the carcass as possible. Pigs do not skin as easily as many other animals, so skinning will leave you with a somewhat ugly finish, but it does save having to scald and scrape.

### Gutting

Once your skin is removed, set the pig to a good working height. Saw through the breast bone. Remove the head by cutting behind the ears at the first joint of the spine.

Cut a bung around the anus, being very careful not to pierce it. Pull up a little of the rectum and tie it off with some string. Now pull the pig up higher.

Slit open the belly from between the hind legs down to the breast bone. It is good to hold the knife in one hand and use the other to hold the guts back. You will really regret it if you pierce them!

Allow the guts to fall into a large bin. You can save the liver and heart if you like. Remember to get the leaf fat for rendering from inside the carcass and around the organs.

Saw through the front of the pelvic bone, and then down through the spine so that you now have two halves. Now you need to chill the pig right down to 4C/40F and hang it there for at least 12-24 hours.

### Dressing/butchering

You can arrange for the local butcher to take over at this point, or you can go on to butcher the pig yourself.

Kunekunes are very fatty and lend themselves very well to bacon and sausages, but the chops and hams are also amazing.

Remove the shoulders cutting in between the third and fourth rib. Cut off the jowl for either jowl bacon or sausages and remove the neck bone from the shoulder.

Cut off the shank just above the knee joint. The shoulder can be cured whole, left as a roast, or boned out. Or you can cut it in half by dividing it between the smallest point of the shoulder blade bone to give  a picnic shoulder (a small ham) and the butt (the body side of the shoulder). Pork butt is actually part of the shoulder, not the ham/back leg.

Remove the hams/back legs by sawing through at right angles to the backbone just in front of the pelvic bone. Remove the shanks by sawing just below the hock.

Now you only have the middle part of the backbone and the ribs. The portion near the backbone is the loin. Separate it from the belly by cutting along a line about a third of the way from the backbone to the bottom of the belly meat. Cut the ribs out of the belly meat, square it up, remove the mammary glands and you can either leave it flat, or roll and tie it ready for curing.

There is also a muscle inside the backbone near the hind end of the loin, this is known as the tenderloin. Remove it and slice it into tenderloin steaks. In Kunkune's it is a small portion, but worth treating with respect as it is quite delicious fried in butter and garlic.

To make chops, cut up between each rib and through the backbone. Otherwise you can bone out the entire loin and cut it into steaks, mince/grind it or turn it into middle bacon.

# Charcuterie

The amazing meat and fat quality of the Kunekune lends itself well to charcuterie. Good quality pasture raised fat lends a wonderful flavour to sausage, bacon and dried meats. There are a huge range of products available to help you get started, from sausage casings to brine mixes, with online sellers offering an array of flavours and accessories. With some easy recipes, basic spice mixes, a mincer and a sausage stuffer you can produce high quality truly 'home made' delicatessen quality sausage.

The real trick to producing good homemade sausages is to keep everything as cold as possible whilst you're making them.

# Simple pork sausage recipe

Makes: 24 classic pork sausages

## Ingredients

900g pork belly

900g pork shoulder

3 tablespoons chopped fresh thyme

3 tablespoons chopped fresh sage

1 tablespoon ground coriander seeds

1/2 teaspoon ground ginger

1/2 teaspoon ground nutmeg

1 tablespoon white pepper

1 1/2 tablespoons salt

110g fine breadcrumbs

2 cloves garlic, minced

3m to 3.5m (32mm) natural hog casings

1. Remove all bones and skin, and roughly chop up the meat. Mince in a meat grinder through a 5mm mincing plate.

2. Combine the pork with the herbs, coriander, spices, seasoning, breadcrumbs and garlic and leave for 2 hours to rest. Meanwhile, soak the hog casings in cold water or as instructed on the packet.

3. Take the mincing blades out of the grinder and attach the sausage funnel.
Slip the end of the wet sausage casing over the attachment and pull the casing down the shaft so that it is bunched up at the base, this is so that you are able to make a good amount of sausages without having to stop and add more casing. Pop the meat back into the grinder funnel.

4. Tie the starting end of the casing into a knot and on the slow setting, gently support the sausage as it is piped into the casing ensuring that it does not pack too tightly and avoid air bubbles.

5. By eye, measure about 4 inches / 10cm per sausage resulting in a yield of about 8 sausages per metre, with extra casing allowance.

6. Squeeze the end of each sausage and twist the casing 2 to 3 times to secure, repeat then tie a knot after the final sausage. Repeat until the sausage meat is used up. Store in the fridge overnight before cooking.

# Simple Bacon recipe

*Homemade bacon is surprisingly easy to make too. Salt, sugar, and an airtight bag is enough to produce bacon in your fridge in around one week. A charcoal grill is one of the easiest things to repurpose as a smoker, or you can buy an actual smoker if this is something you think you will do more often.*

## Ingredients

1.5kg or 3lb skinless, boneless pork belly

3 tablespoons kosher salt

1/3 cup white sugar

2 tablespoons pepper

2 teaspoons paprika

1 teaspoon pink curing salt (aka Prague Powder #1)

apple or cherry wood chunks/chips

1. In a small bowl, combine the pepper, sugar, paprika, salt & curing salt.

2. Place belly on a foil lined tray and pat dry with paper towels. Using half of the cure mix, sprinkle evenly over the surface of the belly, and rub in gently. Turn over and repeat on the other side with the remaining mix.

3. Place the entire belly and curing mix into a large zip top bag and place in the refrigerator for 7 days.  Each day the belly should be flipped onto the other side, and the contents (which will transform to a liquid) should be massaged around the meat.

4. After 7 days, remove from the bag and rinse the bacon under water. Pat it dry with paper towels, and place back in the fridge uncovered (on a rack over a pan to catch any drips) for 24 hours. This will allow it to dry out thoroughly.

5. Smoke the now cured belly using the apple or cherry wood for three hours at 200F or 100 C, or until internal temperature reaches 150F or 65 C.

6. Store bacon in an airtight plastic bag or container in your refrigerator for up to a week, cutting and cooking as required, or wrap it firmly in plastic and store it in your freezer for up to 6 months.

# Breeding

One of the benefits of keeping Kunekune pigs is that they are small enough and friendly enough to be able to keep both boars and sows on your property, which allows you to breed your own.

It is worth saying that breeding any animal should be done with care and consideration. This is especially true when it comes to Kunekunes that have a limited gene pool. Ideally you would get your stock from two different lines and be as unrelated as possible.

Be sure to only breed good, healthy, genetically sound and physically good specimens of the breed.

When selecting breeding stock, look for piglets who are strong and well developed. Short legs, a strong body, a straight back and a 'leg at each corner'. Well developed hams indicate a piglet who has been feeding well from the sow. Size is immaterial at this age but good development is important.

Always choose breeding animals with strong, straight front legs and good feet.

When choosing breeding stock of either sex always check the underline and belly. The position and number of teats is very important in both male and female as the male will pass his teat-traits on to his daughters. They should have 10 evenly spaced teats.

Kunekunes make wonderful pets, but having up to 15 tiny escape artists running around is not for the faint of heart! Be sure that you have the ability to care for the sow and piglets and a way of rehoming the piglets when the time comes.

Pregnant with 15!

## Sow Care

To be able to breed, sows need to be in peak physical conditions both before and during pregnancy and lactation. Overweight sows will struggle to get pregnant and maintain a pregnancy, equally underweight sows will struggle with the demands of pregnancy and lactation.

Choose gilts (unbred females) or sows that are of good conformation, and are physically healthy and well. Put your females into good quality grass and if she is underweight, increase her supplemental feed ration to get her to a good, healthy shape.

Boars usually start to become fertile at about 8 months of age, and they will become fully fertile at about 12 months of age. They do not develop the full secondary boar characteristics, like a thick shield of skin over the shoulders and tusks, until about 18 months of age.

Sows can start to mature at a younger age but ideally should not be mated until at least 12 months of age.

### Heat Cycles

It is usually easy to tell when the sow comes in season. Usually there is a swelling of the vulva and a change in their social behaviour.

Trying to test for "standing heat" by putting pressure on her back to see if she will stand for a mating is not always a reliable sign. Because of their love of scratches, some Kunekunes will stand still whether they are in season or not.

A sow's season lasts for between 8 and 48 hours, and normally occurs every 18 to 22 days until pregnancy occurs.

### Fertility

The average Kunekune litter size is 6 to 8 piglets, although first litters of up to 12 piglets are not unusual. A kunekune may have a litter of up to 16 piglets, but she may need help feeding that many if they all are born alive as most sows only have 10 to 12 teats.

A litter of only 1 or 2 piglets is rare but it does sometimes happen. Usually, if a pregnancy with very few piglets occurs, the sow is likely to reabsorb or abort the litter and start over. As a sow ages, the number of piglets per litter may reduce, but sows can often keep reproducing well up to 8 years of age.

If you try increasing the sow's food intake for up to 2 weeks before mating, it can have a flushing effect on the ovaries and can often increase the litter size.

Sows that repeatedly have small litters, multiple stillbirths or are poor mothers should be culled (not necessarily killed, to 'cull' means to remove from a breeding program), but it is worth noting that often litter size is influenced by environmental factors including the amount or quality of

This pregnancy was just one piglet

feed available or the boar's fertility rather than the sow's genetic makeup.

### Infertility

There are various causes of infertility in Kunekune pigs. The first step to trying to solve the problem is deciding who is at fault, is it the boar or the sow?

A boar's fertility varies during the year, with their fertility being reduced both during very hot weather or very cold weather. Or even a short illness can reduce a boar's fertility for up to 6 – 8 weeks following their recovery.

Sows can demonstrate their infertility in several ways, it may be one or more of the following:

- Failure to come on heat
- Irregular or difficult to detect heat cycles
- Failure to conceive after successful mating.

There are several possible causes of sow infertility, hormonal problems, a reproductive tract damaged by infection, or too fat or too thin in body condition are the common causes.

If a sow has an infertility problem, vet prescribed hormone treatment may sometimes help and might be worth a try in some situations. Often it is a matter of being patient and setting a time limit of 6 to 12 months before deciding to cull from the breeding program and keeping her as a pet, putting her in the freezer, or selling her on as a companion (rather than a breeder sow).

### Signs of Pregnancy

If a sow has been running with a boar for any amount of time, it is possible that she is pregnant. Pregnancy in such a round little pig can be difficult to see until later in the pregnancy.

A pregnant sow will develop a defined milk line later in the pregnancy as her teats begin to swell. In the last days you will be able to express some milk from them.

You may not notice any change at all until the last few weeks until you see the teats developing and the vulva will become larger and more slack towards the end of pregnancy as it gets prepared for birthing.

## Farrowing

### Length of Pregnancy

A pig's gestation is about 116 days in Kunekunes, 2 days longer than most other pig breeds. The common saying is "'3 months, 3 weeks, 3 days" for pigs, but for Kunekunes you need to add 2 more days to that.

## Nesting

It is not uncommon for a sow to start building a nest any time from a few hours to a few days before birth. She will start collecting vegetable matter to make a farrowing area where she feels safe and secure.

Be sure to make sure there is plenty of bedding available for her to use. Options include sawdust, shavings, straw, hay or fleece wool. Wool is not a common choice, but it is an excellent one, especially if she is farrowing in winter. Wool can help keep piglets warm and the wool won't rot easily if it gets wet or dirty and it is a great way to use up fleeces that you might have.

## Farrowing Pens

Farrowing pens vary in design and cost. A simple pig hut will work well as long as it has the following:

- Enough room for the sow to move around and lie down with at least 3ft/1m in front and beside her
- A space all to herself, some sows will share a farrowing hut, but usually this does not go well unless the pigs are already well bonded and the piglets are very close in age.
- Easy human access to reach piglets and clean out as required
- A farrowing rail so that mama cannot squash the piglets against the wall

- A space the piglets can snuggle together away from the sow
- Warm
- Dry
- No drafts
- Heat lamp (if required)
- Plenty of bedding

### *Preparing for Farrowing (birth)*

At least one week before your sow is due to give birth you should transfer the sow to the farrowing paddock or pen. This is the ideal time to deworm her as well. This will lower the stress on her by removing any additional parasites that are also trying to eat the calories that she is consuming.

Farrowing quarters need not be elaborate. A clean, dry, well-bedded and sheltered area is all that is required. A separate pen with a shelter or hut, or a stall in your barn will do quite nicely as the "maternity ward".

For at least the first three to four days it is a good idea to have a board at the bottom of the doorway to keep the piglets contained within the bed and to stop the piglets getting lost. Make sure that the board is not too high, or the sow may have trouble getting over it if her udder is close to the ground.

Be aware of what bowls or puddles of water are around the farrowing pen/paddock as piglets will drown quickly and easily in a surprisingly small volume of water while they are small.

Setting up a heat lamp behind a farrowing rail or "creeper" can help improve piglet survival as it gives somewhere warm to snuggle that is away from the sow which reduces the chance of her lying on a piglet. Kunekunes are usually brilliant mothers, and their smaller size means that a laid on piglet is less like to get squashed, and the mothers do tend to be attentive and will move quickly if a piglet cries out when it gets sat on. However, unfortunately sometimes it does happen, so a farrowing rail can literally be a life saver.

### *Labor and Delivery*

The most reliable way to tell how far off labor is is by feeling the amount of udder development in your sow. As pregnancy progresses, her udder tissue keeps developing, with the teats becoming more prominent as each day passes. In most sows there will be a watery milk able to be expressed from the teats in the last 24 hours of the pregnancy.

The size and consistency of the vulva can also be used as an indication of impending labor. You will notice that the vulva enlarges in both the size and width as the pregnancy progresses, then becomes quite swollen in the last few days before labor starts.

The shape of her abdomen changes in the last few days, and the abdomen hangs much lower to the ground. This is due to ligaments stretching in preparation for farrowing and is commonly referred to as "dropping".

Right at the beginning of labor, a sow may become distracted and restless. She might be getting up and down a lot and find it difficult to get comfortable. Often she will also lose interest in food, although sometimes you might find that she will get up to eat during farrowing when it is feeding time, and then carry on farrowing afterwards.

If she has not already made herself a nest, she might start building one now by gathering up all sorts of vegetation or other things that she finds laying around to build herself a pile to put her back against for farrowing.

The best kinds of bedding to supply her is hay or straw, or raw fleece wool. Wool may sound like a weird option, however it has an advantage in Winter as it helps to keep the piglets warm and it doesn't rot easily if it gets wet or muddy.

The first stage of labor is usually spent pushing or raking material together into a pile/nest. Once a sow has found a space to make her nest, it is terribly difficult to get her to move to a different place, so it is wise to pen her up in a smaller pen with a suitable selter or barn attached before her farrowing time comes.

If you have missed the window and she is lining up to farrow outside, rather than upset her, it is often best to let her farrow outside and then shift her 24 hours later.

Once the contractions of the uterus starts, it puts pressure on the cervix to start dilation. Like humans, the length of time this takes depends on how old the sow is, how many pregnancies she has had before, and what her inherited traits are. A young first timer sow may be in labour for hours before the first sign of a piglet, whereas older sows may only be in active labour for 10 to 15 minutes before piglets start arriving in quick succession. The first material passed during farrowing is often some mucus, some blood spots and/or some piglet faecal material. Once that is passed then the piglet will appear still within the amniotic sac.

Once a piglet is moved into the birth canal it is usually expelled with a few strong pushes from the sow. Usually the umbilical cord will usually break naturally but for any reason that it is either long and dragging, or unbroken you can break it off shorter. Leave at least an inch of cord from the piglets belly button.

Occasionally the umbilical cord will break off very close to the navel of the piglet, which means the cord cannot naturally clamp down to stem the blood supply and the piglet may lose too much blood to survive. If a cord continues to bleed, clamp it between your fingers for 2 to 3 minutes to assist the blood vessels sealing off.

The amount of time gap between delivery of piglets can vary widely, and it does depend somewhat on the age of the sow and the size of the piglets. A sow has two horns to her uterus, which means that as the first horn of the uterus empties, usually there is a piglet every 10-15 minutes then a gap of about half an hour or more, before the piglets from the second horn of the uterus are delivered.

Piglets are often born breech, which means that their back feet present first. This is totally normal and doesn't pose a risk of obstruction.

Once all the piglets are born there is normally a group of placenta that is then passed, which is usually used as a sign that farrowing is finished.

It is quite normal and natural for the sow to eat these, so leave them present for a few hours. If they are still there after 12 hours, take them away and bury or burn them to prevent flies.

### After Farrowing

Once born, a piglet relies on the mother's grunting sounds so that it can find the udder. If your sow doesn't 'talk' much during farrowing, she will sometimes end up with piglets going everywhere. This is an issue because they may end up lost, get chilled and they die quickly in this state. If you can stay with a sow while she is farrowing, it is a good idea so long as she doesn't get upset by too much happening around her.

You can use an old towel to dry each piglet and clear the mouth as it is born, which can help to reduce the chances of hypothermia on a cold night. Most sows that know you well won't mind too much if you need to pick up piglets to steer them in the right direction if they can't find a teat to latch onto but heed her warnings if she is not happy she may bite.

When they are first born piglets are quite uncoordinated, after half an hour or so they gradually get more coordinated and can find a teat themselves.

Within the first 4 hours of birth, your piglets must have colostrum, and preferably within the first hour. It might be safer if your sow is restless during labour to remove the piglets until her farrowing is complete. Place the piglet nearby under a heat lamp until things settle down.

Cold or very weak piglets do best if you take them away from the sow and warm them up elsewhere before returning him to the litter. A squashed piglet seldom survives for very long so if that is the cause of its lack of luster, do not blame yourself for the loss.

### *Winter Farrowing*

Winter farrowing does present its own challenges, but as long as they have access to good shelter, piglets will usually do just fine.

Sows that are close to birthing will seek shelter and start building themselves a nest. If you can pen her up enclosing the farrowing hut, it will limit the strange places she may choose to nest, and also keep out other pigs that might just like the look of her nest as their new sleeping quarters. It also makes it easier to add a heat lamp if necessary.

The biggest challenge with winter farrowing is getting and keeping newborn piglets dry. Adding plenty of dry bedding is your best tool for this. Suitable bedding includes straw, poor-quality hay fleece-wool or baled corn stalks.

Daily removing wet bedding and adding fresh bedding will help to maintain a dry environment for piglets. Young gilts that come from litters successfully raised during the winter months should be considered as sow replacements as they will be hardy and well adapted to the cooler weather, while any animal that doesn't do a good job raising her litter should go on the cull list.

If you have multiple sows farrowing close together, you may find that they litter-share. This is fine, but watch the condition of all the sows to ensure they are getting enough nutrition, especially if one is feeding more than her share of piglets.

## Complications

Kunekune sows are known for their easy pregnancy and births, and their great mothering instincts. However, sometimes things do not go to plan.

### *Stuck Piglet*

 Kunekunes are usually good birthers, and rarely have any problems with farrowing. However, if you notice straining for 30 minutes with nothing passed, it can be a sign of dystocia - a stuck piglet. If this happens, you will need to do an internal examination with a washed lubricated hand, or ring the Vet to come out and see her.

If you reach in you should be able to work with the contractions to reposition the piglet between contractions, and gently help pull with the contractions to help the stuck piglet out.

Oxytocin can be used to stimulate the uterus to contract, but it should not be given without first checking there is no piglet stuck in the birth canal. It is quite common to use this in commercial pigs, however,  it is almost never needed in Kunekunes to assist with birth.

### Piglet born not breathing

If a piglet is born not breathing, try giving it a vigorous rub down with a towel. If this doesn't work, be sure to clear any mucus from its mouth and nose (a bulb syringe works well here) and hold the mouth closed and blow very gently into the piglet's nostrils. In some instances this can save a piglet that would otherwise die.

A piglet born without a heart beat is unlikely to come around, no matter what you do.

### Congenital Abnormalities

Sometimes piglets are born with deformities that are incompatible with normal life, some will die quickly after birth, and others require being put to sleep. These include such things as cleft palate and absence of the anus. Other abnormalities that occur more commonly are umbilical or scrotal hernias which can be fixed easily with surgery, however, these pigs should not be bred from as these conditions are often inherited.

### The Runt

A litter does not always have what could be termed a "runt" but because of the nature of a multiple birth, many litters may have a piglet that has been last at getting the nutrients and is smaller than the others.

Usually, a runt will grow and develop just fine when given ample nutrition. If you can help the runt piglet find its place at the first set of teats right at the beginning, this will be where it is more likely to feed from and it is where the most milk is in most sows. A runt may benefit from topup bottles of a good replacement milk mix once or twice a day.

If you notice a piglet that was "normal sized" when born but is failing to thrive, consider if the sow has enough teats to go around, and if they are all functioning well. Sometimes a sow may have a "dud" teat where there is less milk produced. Treat as you would a runt and offer milk replacement top ups.

### Bottle Raising

Occasionally, a circumstance will arise where you will have to raise a piglet (or several) with a bottle.

The sad reality is that piglets fed from a bottle have a lower survival rate than those raised by their mother, so it is a good thing to take into consideration when deciding whether or not to bottle feed. In the advent of mother death, or too many piglets and not enough milk, you really have no other choice but to bottle feed.

Every baby animal needs colostrum within the first 24 hours of birth. Ideally this would come from the mother, but sometimes this is not a possibility. Bovine (usually cow) or goat colostrum make an OK replacement if you cannot get any pig colostrum.

After 24 hours of colostrum, you can move the piglet on to a bought milk replacement that is designed for piglets.

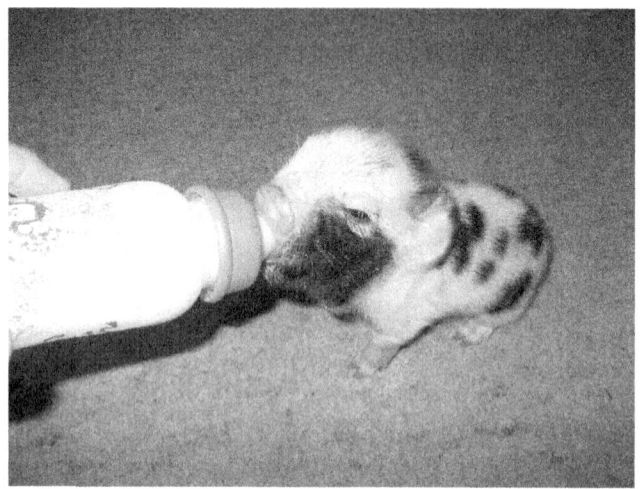

To start with, the small piglets are best fed with a small syringe or eyedropper. Be very slow and careful with this as they can choke easily at this stage. A human baby bottle or an animal bottle with a piglet teat on it is the best thing to move on to after the eye dropper. You can teach them to drink directly from a dish and they are less likely to choke doing this, however it does take them some practise to work it out.

In the first days, the piglets will need fed little and very often, at least every 1 ½ hours. These frequent feeding sessions are vital because this is when they'll be taking in colostrum. Each nursing session will last about five minutes. Make a plan for this first day to be at the piglets' beck and call because this could be the difference between a weak piglet or a healthy, happy, and thriving piglet in the days to come.

Once a milk replacer has been introduced, you can feed them from a bottle every three to four hours. Follow the instructions on the package of milk replacer to know how much to give based on weight to your piglet. In most cases, the babies will lose interest when full, and if they're still hungry, they'll want more. Which is why many people mix up a large batch of milk replacer at once.

It allows you to refill the bottle if needed quickly and easily. Be sure to pay attention to the time frame of the milk replacer because you don't want to feed old milk to a new baby.

From two weeks onwards you can drop their feeds back to 4 times per day, and from 3 weeks you can drop it back to 3 times a day plus some solids. Piglets are usually weaned from the bottle between 5 and 8 weeks.

# Starting on Solids

Piglets will start to eat solids at around 3 weeks of age. To start with they will just steal a little of what their mother is eating, so be sure to add a little extra in increasing volumes as they eat more.

A simple way to add solids is to mix pig feed or pig pellets with some hot water, stir to allow the water to absorb and the feed to cool. Then serve it in shallow pans, they will very quickly work it out. This is also a good time to make sure there is a water station suitable for the piglets to use. A refillable automatic trough is a great option, but shallow water pans are also good as long as they are cleaned regularly and are shallow enough for the piglets to get out of when they climb in them.

### *Weaning*

Breeders vary in what age they wean piglets from their mother at. The ideal is to wean at 6-10 weeks of age, depending on the growth of the piglets and the tolerance of your sow. Once the sow is fighting off the piglets for food, it is a good idea to provide the piglets with food in a separate area that the sow can't get at.

If it is more convenient, you can choose to leave the piglets with the sow, and the piglets will usually wean themselves by 4 months of age.

It is usually a good idea to reduce the sow's food intake once the piglets are weaned or she may become too fat pretty fast. Sows will usually come in season within 1 week of the piglets being weaned off, but it is best to let her have a rest of at least a few cycles before reintroducing her to the boar.

## Castration

Castrating male animals provides many advantages – castrated males can safely be kept with female animals without the risk of unwanted litters, it can potentially reduce aggression in male animals and in those breeds bred for meat, it can reduce 'tainting' of the flesh. Kunekune pigs are no exception, except that maybe entire boars are successfully kept as pets.

The only possible method of castration in pigs is surgical due to their largely internal testicles. Rubber rings and the Burdizzo method (a piece of equipment that crushes the spermatic cord and vessels) are not suitable or legal in most countries to use on pigs.

Surgical castration involves making a small ¾ inch incision over the scrotum with a very sharp blade, through the vaginal tunic grasping the testicle and using a combination of pulling and a twisting motion to remove the testicle and a portion of the blood vessels and spermatic cord in one piece. The wound is left open (not stitched) to heal and an antiseptic spray should also be applied.

In a pig the blood vessels and spermatic cord pass through a hole in the abdominal wall known as the inguinal canal. This little hole can sometimes cause a few problems in both pigs and other animals (including humans). Kune Kune pigs are known to have larger inguinal canals than other breeds, this makes them more susceptible to getting inguinal hernias.

This is when the abdominal contents, usually a loop of bowel, protrude through the inguinal canal and into the scrotal sac. Sometimes the hernia is evident before they are castrated and sometimes it can happen after castration, once the testicles have been removed.

After being castrated, the pigs should be kept somewhere clean and monitored for signs of infection. If there is excessive bleeding, swelling or other concerns a vet should be contacted.

In order to try to prevent a hernia happening after castration, some vets will suture the vaginal tunic closed after removing the testicle. This is known as a 'closed' castration and is recommended by many vets for Kunekunes. Hernias are usually easily repaired with a simple surgical procedure.  As with any operation, there are potential risks such as pain, infection and bleeding when getting a piglet castrated or a hernia repaired.

Opinion varies as to the best age to castrate but generally the earlier the better. Commercial units commonly castrate boars before they are 7 days old, however if you are planning on selling the piglets, many breeders will leave the decision (and cost) of castration to the new owners.

Castration is ideally done around 2-3 weeks of age, somewhere away from their protective mother.. Some vets advocate leaving them until they are around 6 weeks of age which is perfectly acceptable but they will require more anaesthetic and potentially be a higher risk.It is best to check the rules in your country, some will allow you to castrate on-farm up to a certain age, others require anesthetic at any age.

## Vaccination

The most common vaccines used for Kunekunes are Leptospirosis (causes abortion), Parvovirus (causes abortion), and Erysipelothrix (arthritis) every 6 months. Other diseases that can be vaccinated against include E coli scours, Tetanus, Mycoplasma pneumonia, and Haemophilus pneumonia. It is worth checking with your local vet which vaccinations are recommended for your area.

# Drenching

There are 4 types of worms in pigs:

- Intestinal roundworms
- Stomach worms
- Lungworms
- Kidney worms

The most common worms are usually intestinal roundworms in young pigs. Ivomec injection or oral wormers can be used to treat worms. Your vet can advise which is best for your situation.

Piglets should be treated at weaning, 1 month later, then again 3 months later. Adults are ideally treated twice a year, with sows treated pre-mating and pre-farrowing.

# Keeping Kune Kunes with other Animals

Kunekunes are wonderful animals for homesteads, lifestyle blocks, hobby farms or small holdings. Often in this situation, paddock space is at a premium, and animals need to share.

Generally, kunekunes are all too happy to share their space, but the animals that they are sharing with might need some introductory time to allow them to adjust to their smell, sound and behaviour.

There are a few things to consider when combining kunekunes with other animals on the farm.

## Goats or Sheep

Usually given time these will get on just fine. Be aware that a newborn lamb or kid, especially one that is not robust and quick to their feet will look like an enticing snack to your friendly pigs. SO if you are expecting babies, it is best to separate them until the kids or lambs are up and running well.

## Horses

Pigs tolerate horses well, they usually steer clear of their hooves, and don't eat their hay too much. They will tend to spread out the horse manure, making it more difficult to pick up, but spreading it out does make it decompose much faster. Many horses are just terrified of pigs, so be sure to introduce them carefully, and have alternative plans if it doesn't work out.

## Ducks/Chickens

Pigs and poultry go well together if you expect the birds to largely forage for their food. If you plan on feeding them grain, it is best to do it in a way that the pigs cannot get to it or you will find your feed bill climbs steeply and your pigs look very round. Kunekunes will also make short work of any eggs left lying around, and will make a quick snack of baby birds.

## Dogs

Dogs and pigs get on well once they are socialised together. You can even teach them the same commands. Be sure to supervise them closely as they get used to each other.

# Common Questions or Problems

## What is a Kunekune pig's life expectancy?

Kunekunes can be expected to live about 15 years, with some living up to 20 years. With this to consider, if you are keeping your Kunes purely as pets, it is worth deciding if you can commit to this length of time.

Daisy, a few days before she passed age 17+

If you are planning on raising your Kunekunes to butcher, you will usually do this between 9 months and 24 months of age. Older pigs can be used as sausage.

## Can Kunekune pigs live indoors?

Kune Kune pigs are as intelligent as dogs and can easily be trained to go to the toilet outside, as well as other tricks like 'sit', 'roll over' and 'dance'.

Many people are choosing to let their pet Kunes live in the house, with some moving them outside during the night and while the owners are not home. They prefer to be able to move indoors and out during the day, so make sure there is easy access to the outdoors.

Kunekunes are not ideal to keep in a barn without outside time as they are bred to be raised on grazing grass and they will get destructive if they are kept penned up for a long time indoors.

## Irregular Heat Cycles

Pigs can be affected by hormonal issues much like humans can. An overweight or underweight sow may struggle with irregular cycles. Mineral deficiencies or an ovarian growth can also cause this. If your sow is not pregnant within 6 months of running with the boar (especially if he has sired a litter in the past), it is worth getting her checked.

## Pigs Drinking Urine

It is not a pleasant thought, but sometimes (like many other animals) a boar will taste the urine of a sow to check if she is in heat. If you notice your pigs drinking urine, it is also worth checking that they have plenty of fresh water available - is their barrel empty? Is the pig nipple/waterer working? A sodium deficiency can also cause this gross behaviour in pigs. Adding a salt lick to their hut where they can get all the salt that they need can quickly remedy this.

## White discharge with urine

Pigs that have extra calcium in their diet will pass a white chalky or powdery substance from their back end. This is nothing to worry about.

# How to use lard on the homestead

Kunekunes were originally kept as a source of wonderful lard. As a naturally occurring saturated fat, it is solid at room temperature, has a very high smoke point and being grass fed, a really good omega 3 to 6 ratio. Lard is used in traditional recipes, food storage, soap making and, of course, to fry food in.

## Rendering lard

Rendering lard is really very easy. The very best lard is the leaf lard found around the kidneys. However, any fat from your pig can easily be rendered into a beautiful, smooth white lard.

Take the fat that you want to render and cut it into small pieces less than an inch. Remove any meat or other material as best as you can. The smaller you cut your fat, the faster and cleaner it will render. Many choose to run it through a mincer on a large size hole.

There are three options for rendering your lard - on the stove, in the oven or in a crockpot/slowcooker. Place your finely chopped fat into a heavy based pot, casserole dish or slow cooker with about ½ a cup of water to stop it burning until the fat starts to melt. Put it on a low heat and gently cook it out until it stops steaming, meaning the water has all evaporated and then cook it for a further half an hour. Be sure to stir it regularly, and keep the heat on low so that it doesn't brown.

Strain through a sieve into jars to store. The fines can then be crisped up in a pan and eaten as a snack.

## Preserving meat

Preserving meat in lard has been a common practice for centuries, in various forms in many many cultures. You've probably heard of duck confit, but did you know that In French, the word confit means preservation?

A traditional confit method involves salt-curing the meat – usually duck, goose, turkey, or pork – then poaching it in its own fat until it's tender and then storing it covered in that same fat.

Back then, obviously they couldn't refrigerate it, it was just the meat fat that preserved it by keeping out the air and bacteria.

According to old records, a properly confited bird will store in a cool, dry place for 6 months, then you can repeat the process and extend it by another six months if required. Personally, I would struggle with serving this up to the family knowing the risk of botulism. However, I would consider doing it in a pressure canner.

The process is the same for pork or beef. Salt is a powerful preservative that adds flavor as well as protection against bacteria and mold.

**Many old homesteads followed these instructions to store meat in lard. I am not recommending that you try this, but I am providing the instructions for it's entertainment value.**

*"Cook meat as you would cook it for serving. Place it in a dry, sterilized crock and cover immediately with hot lard. Cover with clean wax paper and place on this a crock cover or plate. Store in a cool, dry place. Do not keep meat packed in lard during hot weather unless the storage place is always cold.*

*When meat is removed from the crock, be sure to pack down the remaining meat and cover it again with melted lard so that no air will reach it. It is better to store this meat in small crocks than in large ones, for then it will not be disturbed so often.*

*Roast pork, pork chops, pork steaks, and sausage patties can be cooked and preserved in lard."*

## Making soap

Soap making is an art form all of its own, and I will not attempt to teach you it all in this small section of a book about raising pigs. However, it is worth knowing that once you render your own lard, you can use either the hot process or cold process method to make a solid bar of skin nourishing, gentle, natural soap.

Lard makes a very mild, conditioning soap that is great for your skin. Unlike commercial soaps, where the glycerin is removed and sold as a separate by-product, homemade soap retains the glycerine, which is very moisturising. Lard doesn't lather very well, though, so if you're expecting a bubbly lather from your soap, it's a good idea to add another oil, like a little bit of castor oil or coconut oil (about 5%). Lard on its own makes a great laundry soap for homemade laundry detergent, although we use ours for personal washing and it cleans just fine. It's a very luxurious soap.

Soap is made from lye (otherwise known as caustic soda) which is extremely alkaline. When mixed with water, it causes a chemical reaction that gives off fumes and will burn your skin on contact.

So due care must be taken when mixing the lye and water and making the soap. *Always add your lye to the liquid.* If you pour water into a container of lye, a caustic lye volcano could erupt in your kitchen.

## *Lard and Coconut Oil Soap*

## INGREDIENTS

480 grams lard

120 grams coconut oil

85 grams lye (sodium hydroxide)

228 grams distilled water

*Scent*

(Optional) can be added at trace

20 to 36 grams of your favorite essential oils or fragrance oils (you will need a little over 30  milliliters bottle the equivalent of about one fluid ounce).

*This lard soap recipe makes about 2 pounds of soap which will produce about 6-7 bars of soap.*

## EQUIPMENT

Rubber gloves

Goggles or safety glasses

Digital scale

Thermometer

Glass mixing bowls

Rubber spatula

Measuring spoons

Stick blender

Saucepan

Knife or soap cutter

Mold(s)

Old towels

1. Measure and set aside your essential oils or fragrances and any additives you will be adding

2. Weigh out your lye (sodium hydroxide) in a dry bowl and your distilled water in a large glass bowl. Place your water bowl in the sink.

3. Dissolve the lye (sodium hydroxide) by pouring lye into water distilled water. Make sure that you do this in a well ventilated room or even outside. Take your time to make sure that it is completely dissolved. Let it cool.

4. Weigh out your oils, fats or butters using a digital kitchen scale.

5. Place all of your oils and fats in a saucepan and heat them on low-medium heat. Use your thermometer to monitor that the temperature does not go over 65C/150F.

6. Remove from heat when your oils are between 5060C/120-140F.

7. Monitor the temperature of your lye-water solution with the thermometer. When the lye-solution and the melted oils reach about the same temperature around 40C/100F, add the lye-solution to the melted oils.

8.Use a stick hand blender to mix the soap solution. You should be still wearing your goggles and gloves. Be careful not to splash. Continue to mix until the mixture reaches trace (this means that the mixture has thickened enough that when you drizzle some on the top of the mixture, it leaves a trail (trace) on top, similar to a pudding consistency).

9. Add your additives and scents

10. Blend all these together for a few seconds with a spatula or hand blender.

11. Pour the soap mixture into mold(s). Cover mold(s) with plastic wrap and cover/wrap these with towels for insulation.

12. Let the soap set for 24 to 48 hours or so before taking it out of the mold(s). Unmold and cut the soap into bars using a wire or a soap cutting knife

13. Place the soap bars on a covered rack to dry out and cure for a minimum of 3 to 4 weeks before using them.

You can create your own soap recipes using an online soap calculator like this one: https://www.brambleberry.com/calculator

Feel free to experiment with recipes that you create and use the same cold process instructions above to make your own bars.

## Making salve

Vegetable oils are actually very new on the scene, and humans have been making healing salves with rendered animal fat for many many generations.

A healing salve is a mixture of fats and medicinal herbs that are mixed and used to help treat a specific condition. Using fats or oils with herbs and essential oils (from plants) are a great way to carry the healing properties of the plants because their oils cannot mix with water based mixtures.

The process for making an animal fat salve isn't much different than making any other salve. All you're doing is substituting animal fat in place of some type of vegetable-based oil. The fat can be infused with herbal botanicals, or not, it's up to you. For a basic salve, you mix 1 cup of oil with 1 ounce of beeswax in a double boiler. Heat until the beeswax is dissolved and then pour into tins for use.

One recipe for Farmhouse Herb Salve uses 1lb home-rendered lard and a good handful each of elderflowers, wormwood and groundsel. "Dried herbs can be used but fresh are considered better. This is particularly good as a veterinary aid for softening the udders of newly-calved cows or for sore teats. Its healing properties are remarkable" It also makes a wonderful moisturiser for gardeners hands.

### *Yarrow and Lard Salve*

When used topically, yarrow is said to help heal wounds. It's been used throughout history on boils, sores, cuts, piles, burns, and rashes.

It aids in clotting and decreases the risk for infection due to its antibacterial and anti-inflammatory properties. Perfect to put on insect bites, cuts and grazes.

### INGREDIENTS

1 Cup of rendered lard

1 Tablespoon of Beeswax, grated

1 cup of fresh Yarrow leaves, chopped finely

2-3 drops of lavender essential oil or tea tree oil

## METHOD

1. Warm your lard in a pot over a very low heat until it is liquid. Add your yarrow and stir well.

2. Pour in to a glass jar or stainless steel container that you can cover and place on a sunny windowsill for 2-3 weeks

3. Melt your lard again until it is liquid and strain it through a sieve or piece of muslin. Into a pot.

4. Melt the beeswax in a small pot and add it to the warm lard, heat together over a low heat just until the beeswax is incorporated. Add the essential oils if you please.

5. Pour in a wide mouthed tin and allow to cool.

# Useful websites and Kunekune Associations

The New Zealand Kunekune Association
http://kunekune.co.nz/

The British Kunekune Pig Society
https://www.britishkunekunesociety.org.uk/

American Kunekune Pig Society
http://americankunekunepigsociety.com/

Kunekune Pork Producers Association
https://www.kunekuneporkproducers.com/

Empire Kunekune Pig Association
https://www.ekpa.org/

American Kunekune Pig Registry
http://www.americankunekuneregistry.com/

Printed in Great Britain
by Amazon